EXPEDITION EARTH PRESENTS

MONKEYS

Trivia, Facts and Photos!

Jungle Series

Emma Reed

Expedition Earth is dedicated to
my little explorer, Sofie Lynne

Text Copyright @2013 Emma Reed
All Rights Reserved

Expedition Earth Published by
Thrive Communications & Press
ISBN-13: 978-1482679465
ISBN-10: 1482679469

EXPEDITION MAP

 Fun Monkey Trivia!

The pages ahead are full of fun facts and trivia about monkeys. Just look for the binoculars! If you are ready to test your knowledge now, go to page 35.

YOUR EXPEDITION BEGINS!

Hello Adventurers! Welcome to Expedition Earth. Together we'll discover many amazing places on our planet, and learn about the unique animals that live there.

From giant volcano explosions to whales that weigh 100 tons, our earth has many wonders. Earth is also the only planet known to have life. In fact, there are over 8 million species living on Earth!

Did you know that over half of the Earth's species live in jungles and rainforests? That's amazing! Let's grab our binoculars and take a look. We'll learn about one of the jungle's coolest creatures, Monkeys.

EARTH FACT:

Just like you, Earth has a birthday! On April 22 we celebrate "Earth Day" to appreciate our planet's precious natural environment.

DESTINATION: THE JUNGLE

 TRIVIA: What is the largest rainforest on Earth?

Jungles and rainforests are very similar. They both have high levels of rainfall, and are usually found in warm places like Africa and Australia. Jungles and rainforests have important differences too. Rainforests have thick canopies of tall trees that block out light, while jungles let more light in. The extra light makes plants grow even faster and thicker in the jungle.

The jungle is home to many different types of animals including frogs, insects, tropical birds, snakes and mammals such as jungle cats, monkeys and apes.

ANSWER: The biggest rainforest on Earth is called the Amazon rainforest. It is located in South America, and has the largest collection of plant and animal species in the entire world.

MONKEYS

Photo: Young macaque monkeys with their mother

Monkeys are mammals with long arms and legs. They typically spend most of their life in and around trees!

There are many types of monkeys, over 260 known species in all.

HABITAT

Photo: A dusky leaf monkey sits in a tropical tree

 TRIVIA: What do the fingertips of monkeys and humans have in common?

Monkeys belong to a group of mammals called primates. Primates have large brains and grasping hands. They are very smart and curious – just like you!

There are two types of monkeys: Old World and New World.

"Old World" monkeys live on the continents of Africa and Asia in areas like grasslands, rainforests, and even snowy mountains. They can live in trees or on the ground. They often have pads on their bottoms for sitting. Their tails are not typically able to grasp trees.

"New World" monkeys live in South and Central America, mostly in the trees of tropical jungles and rainforests. Typically these monkeys have tails that can easily hold onto tree branches.

ANSWER: Monkeys have their own unique set of fingerprints just like humans do.

ANATOMY

Photo: Spider monkey wraps his tail around a tree to relax

Monkeys have bodies that are similar in many ways to humans. They have arms, legs and thumbs that can move easily. They also have flexible limbs for grasping and climbing.

Monkeys come in many different colors of fur including black, brown, white or gray. Some even have orange, blue, yellow or red fur!

SIZE

**Photo: A tiny pygmy marmoset perched
on a branch in the Amazon**

 TRIVIA: What is the smallest monkey species?

Monkeys come in many shapes and sizes. The smallest monkeys are less than six inches long and weigh less than a can of soup. The biggest monkeys can weigh more than 100 pounds.

ANSWER: The smallest monkey is the pygmy marmoset, a New World monkey. Adults weigh just 3 to 5 ounces. Meanwhile the largest monkeys are baboons and mandrills. They are Old World monkeys and can weigh up to 120 pounds!

FEEDING

Photo: A macaque monkey eating a plant

 TRIVIA: What is the term for the type of diet a monkey has?

Monkeys like to eat plants like flowers, herbs, roots, fruit and leaves. They also eat animals like insects, birds or reptiles. Sometimes they even eat dirt!

Monkeys like to drink water, and can use a leaf to scoop up water like a cup.

Most people picture bananas when they imagine a monkey eating. It's true that monkeys eat bananas, but they do not like the skins. Instead, they peel the bananas first with their fingers or toes and throw the skins aside.

ANSWER: Most monkeys are *omnivores*. This means they have a diet with a variety of plant and animal food.

COMMUNICATION

Photo: A tufted capuchin monkey makes a face

TRIVIA: If you see a monkey grinning, is he happy or mad?

Monkeys are a very smart species. For example, they have been known to make tools out of sticks and rocks.

Monkeys like to communicate with each other through sounds, body movements, and the faces they make. Monkey groups can get very loud as they whistle, chirp, chatter and howl.

Sometimes monkeys get angry with each other. Staring is thought to be a threat. A monkey will often look away when he wants to avoid a fight.

ANSWER: Showing teeth is a sign of aggression or being angry, even when it looks like a monkey is grinning!

MOVEMENT

Photo: A young spider monkey walks on its hind legs

 TRIVIA: What is the fastest monkey?

The movement of monkeys is called "locomotion". While they aren't as fast as a train, most monkeys are able to move at very quick speeds. Using their feet, hands and tail, monkeys can move on the ground and through trees.

Monkeys can grasp, climb and leap with their strong fingers and toes.

Most monkeys have long tails. Some monkeys can hang from their tails and even use their tail like an extra hand. Some monkeys walk on all fours, but some can also walk and leap on two legs.

ANSWER: The quickest monkey is the patas. They are large monkeys with long, slender limbs. Patas monkeys have been recorded at 34 miles per hour!

MONKEY GROUPS

Photo: A group of baboons roams together in the African bush

TRIVIA: What are groups of monkeys called?

Social life is important for monkeys. They like to bond by eating and sleeping close to each other.

Monkeys like to live in groups. Some monkey groups are small and have only a few males, females and their infants. Other monkey groups grow as large as several hundred monkeys.

Young monkeys like to play together and sometimes pretend to fight. Grown monkeys help each other look for food.

Groups of monkeys also help protect each other from dangers.

ANSWER: Groups of monkeys are called troops or tribes.

BABY MONKEYS

**Photo: A baby rhesus macaque monkey
rides on its mother's back**

 TRIVIA: What are baby monkeys called?

Baby monkeys are usually born one at a time, though the marmoset and tamarin species often have twins and triplets.

Baby monkeys are born with their eyes open and have hair. Sometimes their fur is a completely different color than their parents.

Infant monkeys are helpless at birth. They get rides by clinging to their mothers or fathers, and also drink milk from their mother.

Baby monkeys are very active, and spend most of their waking hours playing with other monkeys and eating. Sometimes older monkeys even help "babysit" young monkeys.

ANSWER: Baby monkeys are called infants. You were an infant once too! Have you seen pictures of yourself as an infant? Did you look like your mom or dad?

LIFESPAN

Photo: A mandrill sits on a tree branch

 TRIVIA: The mandrill has the longest lifespan. How many years can they live?

The lifespan of monkeys depends on the species, but monkeys can live very long lives. Wild monkeys can live about 15 to 20 years on average.

Monkeys face risks in their lives including having their homes – the jungles – destroyed, or being harmed by people hunting for monkeys.

ANSWER: The mandrill can live up to 45 years in the wild!

GROOMING

**Photo: Line up everyone! Rhesus monkeys help
each other scratch and groom**

Monkeys like to groom each other every day. They help each other get rid of dirt and bugs to stay healthy and clean.

Grooming is also a way of bonding with each other. Some monkeys have even been seen grooming as a way to make up with a friend after a fight.

TYPES OF MONKEYS

There are hundreds of monkey species – from lovable and cute to amazing and weird! Let's take a look at some of the world's favorite monkeys.

Proboscis

TRIVIA: What does the word "proboscis" mean?

The proboscis monkey is also known as the long-nosed monkey. It is a reddish-brown Old World monkey found in Asia. They live in trees near rivers and swamps.

The big noses help male proboscis monkeys make loud honking sounds. The females have smaller noses.

Proboscis monkeys climb and jump in the trees. They use their long tails for balance. They also like to leap from the trees into rivers. They have slightly webbed feet that can paddle through the water. They also have big bellies that can slowly break down their food.

ANSWER: Proboscis means "long nose" – the perfect name for this big-nosed monkey!

Rhesus

 TRIVIA: Monkeys have been to space – True or False?

Rhesus monkeys are one of the most familiar monkey species. They are brown monkeys with red on their faces and rears.

The rhesus monkey is found in Asia. However, a few troops have now been introduced in the wild in Florida (the United States). The rhesus monkey is very smart and can live well in human communities. They are very social monkeys, and love to make loud noises.

They are very good climbers and swimmers. They eat roots, fruit, seeds and bark, as well as some small animals.

ANSWER: True! Even before humans went to space, the rhesus monkey did! Between 1948 and 1961, several countries around the world, including the United States, sent monkeys into space.

Golden Lion Tamarin

 TRIVIA: Some monkeys are *endangered*. What does that mean?

Golden lion tamarins get their name from the beautiful gold manes that surround their face. They are rare and endangered monkeys that live in the coastal forest region of Brazil.

The lion tamarin typically has twins or triplets when their babies are born. The father helps the mother by carrying the infant around between feedings.

Golden lion tamarins live mostly in trees. They have very long fingers that help them travel around on branches and catch insects, fruit and other small animals to eat.

ANSWER: *Endangered* **means an animal is at risk of becoming extinct. If an animal becomes "extinct" there would be no more of that animal living on Earth.**

Capuchin

Capuchin monkeys are small and quick monkeys that live in Brazil and other parts of Latin America. They typically live in large groups in the jungle.

The fur of a capuchin is light tan around the face, neck and shoulders. The rest of its coat is dark brown. It has a long tail covered in fur that they use to wrap around tree branches.

Capuchin monkeys can jump nine feet, and they use this motion to move easily from tree to tree. They are very good at catching frogs and cracking nuts. They also eat fruit, insects, leaves and small birds.

The capuchin is known as a very small and cute monkey. They are also very clever and easy to train. For this reason they are popular with humans for pets and entertainment.

Squirrel Monkey

The squirrel monkey is a small New World monkey found in jungles of Central and South America. Even though they are tiny, they have a very long tail. Their tail cannot grasp branches. Instead, the squirrel monkey uses its tail for balance while climbing around.

Squirrel monkeys have very colorful fur. It is mostly short with olive and gray color, but their legs are bright yellow and they have white faces. They also have a tuft of longer, darker hair on their small heads.

The squirrel monkey likes to live in thick forest areas that are close to streams for safety. They are very social and can live in troops of 500 monkeys! The troops sleep together at night, but break up into smaller groups during the day to find food.

Squirrel monkeys are also very smart – one of the smartest monkey species in the world. They also have great eyesight and color vision, which means they can easily find food even in the thickest forest.

Howler Monkey

Howlers are New World monkeys that live in tropical Central and South America. They are the largest of all New World monkeys. They also have a tail that can wrap around branches. This means that even though they are very large, they spend most of their time up in the trees. They rarely come down to the ground.

These monkeys are named for their very loud howling cries. When many howlers make noise together they can be heard up to three miles away! They usually make noise to warn other monkeys to stay away from their group.

Howler monkeys have beards with long, thick hair. Their hair is usually black, brown or red. They eat mostly leaves, and spend their time munching on greens up in the trees.

Mandrill

Mandrills are the largest of all monkeys. They are also very shy. Mandrills live only in the rainforests in Africa. They spend most of their time on the ground, but can also climb trees. They eat plants and animals.

Mandrills are very colorful, with blue and red skin on their faces, as well as bright colored rumps. These colors get even brighter when a mandrill becomes excited.

Baboon

 TRIVIA: Why do baboons climb up trees and cliffs at night?

The baboon is one of the biggest monkeys in the world. Most baboons live in the grasslands of central and southern Africa. Baboons live in groups of about 50 monkeys.

A baboon has big ears, a large snout and small eyes. They can move around well on ground, and can also climb trees. There are five different types of baboons. They all look very similar, but have different colored hair. Most male baboons have furry manes that cover their shoulders.

A baboon mostly eats grass and plants, but sometimes they eat other small animals. Their favorite food is fruit. They like to fill their cheeks with fruit so other monkeys cannot take it away.

ANSWER: Baboons climb up cliffs and trees at night to keep out of danger.

Woolly Monkey

Woolly monkeys live in rainforests in South America. They spend most of their time in trees, often hanging from their long strong tails. Just like their name, woolly monkeys have thick, woolly fur.

One of the most amazing things about woolly monkeys is that they can walk on two legs, just like you! Woolly monkeys live in groups, and together they look for food and play in trees.

Colobus Monkey

 TRIVIA: Colobus monkeys have three types of calls - What are they?

The anatomy of the colobus monkey is part of what makes it so special. Unlike other monkeys, the colobus monkey does not have thumbs.

Colobus monkeys have beautiful black fur that stands out against a long, white mane, whiskers and beard. They also have a bushy white tail.

Colobus monkeys live in forests in Africa. They often like to hide in bamboo. They stay mostly stay in trees, rarely coming down to the ground. They like to leap up and down with their arms and legs held out to grab the next branch. Their long hair and tails are believed to act like a parachute during these long leaps.

Colobus monkeys only eat leaves. They have strong stomachs that let them eat dangerous plants that other monkeys cannot eat.

ANSWER: The colobus monkey makes a song call, a warning call, and a mating call. Local people say that colobus monkeys are good weather forecasters because they often become quiet when bad weather is on its way.

Monkey Trivia
Test your monkey knowledge!

Q: What do the fingertips of monkeys and humans have in common?

Monkeys have their own unique set of fingerprints just like humans do!

Q: What is the smallest monkey species?

The smallest monkey is the pygmy marmoset, which is a New World monkey. Adults weigh just 3 to 5 ounces. Meanwhile the largest monkeys are baboons and mandrills. They are Old World monkeys and can weigh up to 120 pounds!

Q: What is the term for the type of diet a monkey has?

Most monkeys are *omnivores*. This means they have a diet with a variety of plant and animal foods.

Q: If you see a monkey grinning, is he happy or mad?

Showing teeth is a sign of aggression or being angry, even when it looks like they are grinning!

Q: What is the fastest monkey?

The quickest monkey is the patas. They are large monkeys with long, slender limbs. Patas monkeys have been recorded at 34 miles per hour!

Q: What are groups of monkeys called?

Groups of monkeys are called troops or tribes.

Q: What are baby monkeys called?

Baby monkeys are called infants.

Q: The mandrill has the longest lifespan. How many years can they live?

The mandrill can live up to 45 years in the wild!

Q: What does the word "proboscis" mean?

Proboscis means "long nose" - the perfect name for the big-nosed monkey!

Q: Monkeys have been to space - True or False?

True! Even before humans went to space, the rhesus monkey did! Between 1948 and 1961, several countries around the world, including the United States, launched monkeys into space.

Q: Some monkeys are *endangered*. What does that mean?

Endangered means an animal is at risk of becoming extinct. If an animal becomes "extinct" there would be no more of that animal living on Earth.

Q: Why do baboons climb up trees and cliffs at night?

Baboons climb up trees and cliffs at night to keep out of danger.

Q: Colobus monkeys have three types of calls - What are they?

The colobus monkey makes a song call, a warning call, and a mating call. Local people say that colobus monkeys are good weather forecasters because they often become quiet when bad weather is on its way.

ABOUT THE AUTHOR

Emma Reed grew up romping through salamander-filled streams and canoeing past crocodiles, but found her life's work in putting pen to paper as an internationally-published writer. Yet it was her children who inspired her to launch her most exciting venture, Expedition Earth. Through the Expedition Earth series, Emma combines her passion for nature with her love for education and literature. Her ongoing inspiration is seeing the spark of curiosity and awe in a child's eyes when they've learned something new about our amazing Earth. Emma lives with her family in Georgia. She can be reached at **expeditionearthbooks@gmail.com**.

Did You Know?

There are more animal books in the Expedition Earth series!

**Visit emmareed.info
to start a new adventure.**

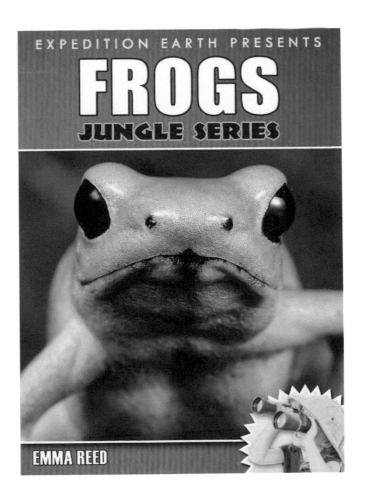

27641292R00024

Made in the USA
Lexington, KY
18 November 2013